GW00391488

About the Authors

Jane Franklin is a primary school teacher and mother to three grown up children. She initially trained to teach children with special educational needs; never realising that one day her second child would give her all the training she needed.

James Franklin is now in his early twenties. After struggling with his emotions as an autistic child, he has now followed his passion to work as a Groundsman both at an independent school and at Wembley Stadium. His ambition is to one day work for a top football club.

Dedication

To Mum/Granny. For your guidance and inspiration that never ends xx

Jane and James Franklin

18 SUMMER HOLIDAYS, 18 YEARS TO GROW

AUSTIN MACAULEY
PUBLISHERS LTD.

A CIP catalogue record for this title is available from the British Library.

ISBN 9781786127730 (Paperback)
ISBN 9781786127747 (Hardback)
ISBN 9781786127754 (E-Book)

www.austinmacauley.com

First Published (2017)
Austin Macauley Publishers Ltd.
25 Canada Square
Canary Wharf
London
E14 5LQ

In memory of Mum/Granny, Aunty Joan, Uncle Jack, Rachel and Grandad Franklin.

'Life's a Beach'

Those were the words on one of James's favourite holiday t-shirts. I always felt this t-shirt was particularly appropriate for James as for him, life had, at times, been an absolute bitch.

Summer

Clear skies, clear waters, clear mind. These are the reasons I only ever write while I am on my summer holiday. And there also lies the reason for this book taking so long to write.

Maybe it's feeling at one with nature, sitting on the beach, looking out to sea, listening to the trickling (some years crashing) waves, and the rustling trees. These are the times when my mind feels free; away from the hustle and bustle, the stresses and strains, the deadlines and duties of everyday life. I finally have time with my family, time to refresh, time to think and be creative. Summer holidays see the real me before I get swallowed up again by school work, homework, clock watching and that overwhelming feeling of there is always something to do, always somewhere to be.

Our summer holiday is a time when we sit and talk and reminisce. And so, the many chats with James about his views on life have come about. And his views and reflections have matured with each summer holiday.

This book tells you no more than our story; how a sometimes difficult child has grown into a mature young man. It tells you about the problems we faced on our journey. But, more importantly, James gives you an insight into how growing up with autism has felt from his point of view.

The Panini Moment

Before embarking on this book, we had enjoyed many wonderful and eventful holidays with James. To recall just a few, there was the Isle of Wight holiday when we watched one ferry leave as we waited for ours. James was convinced this was our ferry (he has never been good at waiting), and subsequently had the biggest screaming meltdown known to mankind. And all this happened in the back of our car in a queue surrounded by other cars. This may well be the reason why we did not dare to attempt airports until this year. Imagine watching all those planes take off coupled with the possibility of delays!

There were other holidays where he totally immersed himself in wet sand, where he became overwhelmed with the seaside noises and reacted in a way that deafened out these sounds, or the numerous times when he refused to walk any further. The list is endless.

Then there was the Panini moment (as it came to be known); the moment that finally inspired me to start writing about James again. It was August 2006. After spending a beautiful summer's day at La Palmyre on the west coast of France, Daniel, James's older brother, eagerly went to the main bar where they were showing a football match between Arsenal (Dan's team) and Manchester City. Dan kindly said to James "If Arsenal win, I will buy you a Panini." And he would, in time, buy James a Panini.

Arsenal did win and straight after the match had finished we went into the nearest town to a Pizzeria for our evening meal. All was well. However, immediately after we had finished our meal and the bill was being paid, James asked for his Panini. He had just eaten a large pizza but, from his point of view, Dan had promised him a Panini. Arsenal had, after all, won their match; therefore, in James's mind, it was Panini time! And so it began! We obviously said 'No' to the Panini. Dan could get it the next day. But no, we were asking James to wait and more importantly go against what he had been promised. There was no reasoning with him. His explosive mood lasted for two days when we finally said he could have the Panini.

You may well wonder why we did not just give in for an easy life. Yes, that would have solved the problem at that time, but I wonder what we would be left with now. An instant easy life would not, I feel, have led us to the position we are in now.

Giving in to James throughout his life may well have led to an easier time all round as we faced each day. However, it is standing our ground and challenging him to try new experiences which has led us to the well-rounded more confident adult we have today. Ultimately the best resources we ever had for bringing up James were Daniel and Becky. James had to fit in with our family, not everyone fit in with James!

And so I started writing again, really just as a way of getting my thoughts and feelings out. And on the next year's holiday, I wrote some more and so the story goes. James then became interested in what I was writing. He had often become frustrated that people did not understand what it was like to be him. This seemed a good way of sharing his thoughts.

When James was 17 I asked him to think about what he hoped to achieve by writing this book. This was his response:

'I just want my friends from primary school to know what I was going through. How they must remember me and the person I am now are very different. There are only really 3 people I still see from my school and they are people I grew up with from when I was very small and my mum still sees their mums. No one else has kept in touch, but I hope now that they read this they will find out who I really am and what was happening when all they saw was probably a strange little boy'.

Why This Year?

So why have we finally got to the point of rounding this book off this year? We could have carried on writing for another few years of holidays. I suppose we are at a point where we can bring things to a close, or at least bring this chapter of James's life to a close. James is now 18 and I now know that the years of hard work, pain, tears, and anxiety have all paid off. What a transformation into the well-rounded, mature, and hard-working 18 year old I now have. I am so proud of my family. All three are loving and caring, and after years of James tormenting Becky, they are now larking about in the sea together. Daniel has been a superb role model to James and has enabled him to test the waters with the safety of an assured friend by his side. Their friendship and bond is something I love to see.

The other reason is that too much has happened to make me think 'seize the moment, life is too short'. In the last few years too many special people have passed away – my mum, my Aunty Joan and Uncle Jack, and now, this summer, my cousin Rachel. Enough to make me think that life is for living and that achievements are not work related, they are life related. My greatest achievement is my family. And the thing I love doing but never have time for is writing. So … it's time to start writing about my family!

Was This Meant to Be?

I am a firm believer in fate and truly feel that 'all things happen for a reason' whether we like them at the time or not. The phrases 'whatever will be, will be', and 'it's written in the stars' are beliefs that I hold dear.

And so, I often look back at a conversation I had with my friend, Niki, not long before my wedding in 1989. Niki was to be my bridesmaid. We had become good friends while we were both training to be teachers specialising in The Education of Children with Special Educational Needs.

While putting the world to rights, we pondered on the thought 'Do you ever wonder if someone up there (pointing to the clouds) will think that if we enjoy working with children with special needs, then perhaps we should, in fact, be given a child with a special need?' I forget now who posed the question. It was probably a silly thought, I know. We dwelt on the subject for some time and then the thought passed.

At that point in time 'special needs' meant 'handicap' to us. We had been trained to view special needs under an array of labels and the road to inclusion had only just begun. The Warnock Report (1978) had led to the 1981 introduction of the Statement of Special Educational Needs with parents being given new rights and a legal change in categorisation. Labels such as profound learning difficulty, severe learning difficulty, moderate learning difficulty and emotional and behavioural difficulty were the terms that we were working within at this point in time. At the time of our conversation I wanted to work with children with severe learning difficulties and Niki wanted to work with children with profound difficulties. Our training had covered all aspects. We thought we knew many of the facts, the teaching methods, the curriculum, and so on. However, there was much we did not yet know.

Little did I know at that time, that one of my own children would have special educational needs and no amount of training to teach such children would ever prepare me for being the parent of such a special child. I knew nothing of the emotions involved, the frustration, the attitudes of others, or the numerous brick walls we would meet along our way. Equally I did not know how much the experience of being the mother to such a special individual would change me and mould me into the person I am now.

Settling Down

Life was quite smooth for the next few years. Phil and I had a lovely wedding day and a week before the big day I got my first teaching job. That was the first change in my plans. Having set my heart on teaching children with severe learning difficulties, there were simply no jobs on offer at the point of me qualifying. Well, in reality there were jobs but not within a distance that I could easily access. Instead I responded to an advert for a mainstream reception class teacher, something I had never previously considered. The advert said 'we are 24 little children who really need a teacher for September'. How could I resist? Well quite easily really as I had no idea what to do with mainstream reception class children, but, somehow, I got the job. I was later told by one of my colleagues that as it was nearing the summer holidays and the time to employ someone was ticking away, I would basically have been given the job anyway as long as I could breathe! I think he was joking, but hey who knows.

Despite my reservations, I loved my new job. It was a lovely friendly school despite being in a difficult area and the intake brought its own share of children with special needs so I still felt in some way my training was being used. After some time, I applied for an in-house promotion which not only provided me with a small financial bonus but also enabled me to liaise with the Infant Speech and Language Unit being set up in the school grounds. Again, I thought this was how my training would be used.

I grew to love teaching Reception class. In my second year, I was joined by a Nursery Nurse, Jo, who became a very good friend. In those first few years after having James, Jo proved to be one of the few people who would listen to me talking about him and his problems. At work Jo and I always had plenty of giggles and so things remained the same until 1992 when I fell pregnant with Daniel. I left work at the Christmas of 1992 and Daniel was born in March 1993. Life greatly changed at that point. Daniel was beautiful, blond, and I had no intention of ever returning to work.

Daniel grew up to be well-behaved, hard-working, calm and quiet. All these qualities helped to pave the way for James bursting onto the scene. Had James been my first child I think people may have had a harsher attitude towards us. It would most definitely have been 'the parents fault' if James had come first. Daniel gave us a little bit of street cred that proved we were capable of bringing up a lovely, well-behaved child.

James Enters the Scene!

On 15th May 1995 James was born. He was just lovely; 7lb 3½ ounces and perfect, another blond little boy. We were so happy. As much as other people may have wanted me to have a girl at that point, I was really happy with another boy – a brother for Dan. Once again, we marvelled at the miracle of birth. We were so lucky, once again, to have a perfect child.

We had a very easy first year with James, only interrupted by Dan's (not so terrible) twos. But James himself was no trouble. Everyone commented on what a placid baby he was.

James did not eat quite as heartily as Dan but Dan had been an exceptionally good eater so we could not really compare. He would gag on his food at times though. This became a bigger problem for him as he grew a little older, as particular textures seemed to trigger this response in him. He was also slightly later to crawl at about 11 months. Again, this did not seem anything to worry about. As everyone said, he is a second child. He doesn't need to get going. Dan will get everything for him.

At 8 months old, James had his developmental check. Everything was fine, except that he did not pass his hearing test. We weren't too worried as so many children fail at this age due to colds and snuffles and he was quite snuffly!

However, James failed the hearing test two more times and so was referred to see an audiologist.

And so, in many respects, begins the story of James ...

From this point on James failed all his hearing tests. His hearing was always down, or he could not locate the sound. Flat traces were recorded and we were told that James had Glue Ear.

However, we were also told to wait. It would probably go of its own accord. Many children have Glue Ear at some point in their lives it is true and the audiologist did not like inserting grommets.

And so we waited. Meanwhile, James continued to fail his hearing tests and had continued ear infections, causing him a great deal of pain. We became a regular at the doctor's and James started trying out a variety of different antibiotics. We unwittingly pumped these into him.

Looking back now, I feel angry at what we didn't do during this time, but like any naïve parents you and I are in the hands of the medical profession and believe that the professionals know what they are talking about and trust that they know best. Hindsight really is a wonderful thing!

It was also at this point that other problems started to emerge. James seemed to crawl forever. The skin on his knees was quite hard from all the wear and tear. It was not until he was seventeen and a half months old that he finally got up on his feet and walked around. Even then, he really did not like to walk for long. Even at the age of three and four, his stamina was poor and he wanted to be carried if he walked any distance.

It also became clear that James was slow to start talking and with this the effects on his behaviour became apparent. Coincidentally this was also around the time of his MMR inoculations. I have my own opinions on this. Only to say that many changes came to light with James from this point forward. James was very physical, always hitting and slapping for no apparent reason. He started to have regular tantrums, again not so unusual. He was approaching the terrible twos after all.

We started taking James to Tumble Tots™, a physical activity program for toddlers. We thought that maybe this would channel some of his energy. Daniel had attended for quite some time and really enjoyed the sessions. James did not last long at Tumble Tots. He found it difficult to balance and to climb high, and to generally follow instructions. He really did not like the noise level in the big hall, although this would have been tolerable to you or me.

Sometimes James would just stand in the middle of the room and scream, to the gaze of the many onlookers with their supposedly perfect and very precious children. I began to dread Fridays. Neither James nor I were enjoying the forty-five minute session, and so a bout of illness with ear infections gave us our timely way out.

Something is Not Quite Right

Little had changed by the Christmas of 1997, except that James's behaviour had become increasingly worse with more tantrums and more aggression. His speech was still delayed and we had begun attending speech therapy with him. His appointments were irregular; 3 or 4 months apart and in the last year the therapist changed three times. How could anyone possibly know James from a few notes and a 20 minute session? As such, we weren't really told anything we didn't already know.

That Christmas was one of the turning points in James's life, or so we thought. His behaviour was awful that Christmas. The more people that were in our house, the worse it was – aggressive, screaming, the pattern emerges. A few days after Christmas James became really poorly. The next day his ear was oozing with gunge. On visiting the doctor, we discovered that he had a perforated ear-drum.

As hard as this was to see James suffering so much, suddenly people took notice of him. He was sent for another hearing test, failed, and was immediately sent to the Ear, Nose and Throat consultant. With severe glue ear in both ears, he was admitted to have grommets inserted in April 1998, a few weeks before his 3rd birthday.

Though a seemingly minor operation in the great world of operations, this was, we hoped, a big day for James.

So many people told us of their children having grommets and of the difference they had seen in only a few weeks, not only in their hearing but also in both their speech and behaviour, too. This was, we thought, the end to our troubles and James's life could finally really begin.

Before I had it done, I was playing with a few people. The consultant was the one with the disc light on his head. When he actually gave me the grommets, they were quite a cool possession to keep.

James seemed so vulnerable in hospital, dressed in his gown and reaching out to me as the mask went on him and he went under the anaesthetic. Forty-five minutes later he emerged, slightly blood-stained and moaning in his sleepy state. He looked even more vulnerable than when he went in. Grommets had been inserted in both ears and his adenoids had been removed. However, there was a sense of relief that came over me as I felt that now, just maybe, his problems were over.

James recovered quickly from his operation and later that day I brought him home, expecting to see changes in him over the next few weeks. There were no real changes. James's speech did improve over time but within a week of being in hospital, he had another ear-infection.

Six weeks after the operation, we returned to the hospital for James's check-up. There we met a fellow patient from when he was in hospital. The mother told me of the vast improvement in the speech and temperament of her son. We could not report the same.

We took James into the consulting room for his check-up. He had another ear-infection and his right grommet had already moved out of position. (Grommets usually stay inserted for between 6 and 18 months).

So what now?

Into the Mix

James's operation had unfortunately coincided with him starting playgroup. He had been for his initial visit but then totally missed the staggered start as the removal of his adenoids meant that he had to keep away from potential infection (i.e. other children) for a couple of weeks.

It was very difficult leaving James each morning. There would be tears, screaming and more. This did not seem too unusual as he had been thrown straight into playgroup once everyone else had already settled. We went back to staggering him, half an hour one day, one hour the next, two the next until he stayed for 3 full hours without too many problems. He would, however, still lapse into bad days from time to time.

James continued to have ear-infections throughout his time at playgroup. He liked playing boisterous games but had no or little interest in books, puzzles, drawing, etc. He was often sent out at story-time because he could not sit still or pay attention.

The helpers reported that he would often look right through them when they were talking to him and that he could not follow instructions. His name would often be called first when I came to meet him, but James was still one of the last out and I invariably had to send him back to get his bag.

The same was true at home. James would not attempt puzzles and, even if persuaded, he showed a lack of spatial awareness.

James could not settle to any activity for long but flitted from one to another. His concentration span was short and he was often noisy when he was playing. He did not engage in solitary imaginative play. He did, yes, play with the construction vehicles, but on closer scrutiny, lined these up in the same way around the car mat each time he played with them.

James remained a very physical child. He loved being outdoors and was constantly covered in bumps and bruises. He could easily trip over nothing and walked into objects which were avoidable.

Playgroup

At play group, I used to play with Heather. She is the only person I remember playing with. And I remember story-time at the end of the morning. I didn't really like it though.

There were odd times when I used to get scared. That was mainly because my mum wasn't there. I remember at playgroup there was a tiger book. I think it was 'The Tiger Who Came To Tea'. I thought the tiger was at the door. I was really fidgety because I was scared but I probably got told off because they thought I wasn't sitting still.

Attitudes

Perhaps now I should take a moment to discuss the attitude of other people I have met along the way. I could write chapters on this subject.

Daniel was now at school so James had chance for a run around in the playground each morning and afternoon at drop off and pick up time. James became a source of entertainment to Daniel's friends. They quickly learned that if they teased James or poked or prodded him, he would easily become wound up and lash out at them. This was great fun for the older children. It was so easy to get James into trouble.

I am not apportioning blame – believe me. James could just as easily get himself into trouble. He would push and hit and generally aggravate and have some quite wonderful tantrums, but their additional provocations only made the situation worse.

It came to the point where James was getting the blame for everything, no matter what. Another child could push James and nothing was said, but if James pushed back, a big deal would be made of it. I would hear the sighs and tutting and see the condescending looks.

James's retaliations were often, of course, worse than the initial provocation. He was a very strong and robust little boy and the other children were not always quite so strongly built. I had no qualms about James being told off, if the other children were as well. But what message was being given to James? It was fine for others to aggravate him, but a crime for him to do the same.

At this point I discovered that I really could not be bothered with some of my supposed friends especially when I overheard two of them talking and saying what a horrible boy he was. I bit my lip as ever, and put on a smiley face. Very few 'friends' actually took any interest in the underlying causes of James's behaviour and asked questions. Most were just too quick to judge.

Can I blame them? I don't think I can. I too have been guilty of making snap judgements on children I have seen. You know, the ones in the supermarket causing all kinds of mayhem. 'What a naughty child!', 'It must be the parents' and so on.

If any good has come of this, I hope my own attitude has changed. Children are not born badly behaved. We should not make snap judgements based on the symptoms but stop and think and look at the underlying causes. A greater understanding is needed all round and this can only be achieved through greater knowledge. But even when I tried to tell friends about James's problems, very few have really taken time to listen. I hope this book might achieve more.

Big School

In January 1999 James started Nursery at Daniel's school. On the home-visit before he started I presented the Nursery teacher and Nursery Nurse with an outline of James's ear, speech and behaviour problems so far. I warned of the behaviour changes in the build up to an ear infection. I am glad I did this as, before long, the picture came true.

James's first week at Nursery went well but he then digressed into tearful starts each morning. The teacher carried out baseline assessments on the children in their first few weeks. I was called in because James's score was so low. I think the teacher thought me strange when I said I was glad that I had been called in. I knew James had problems. It was a relief to me that the school also recognised these problems so early in his school life. James was to continue to be assessed and more specific work would be done with him.

Before long James had another ear-infection. His behaviour became increasingly worse that week; he grabbed the neck of one of his peers during story-time. James continued to have ear-infections for the remaining winter and spring months. He was regularly on antibiotics and his behaviour remained erratic.

As for his ability, James's fine-motor skills were poor although by the end of his time in Nursery, he had become a whizz with scissors (as many items in our house soon discovered). James was still unable to sit still for story times. He showed little interest in pencil activities or in puzzles. He began to enjoy books especially if they had amusing pictures. His role-play was also poor. He lacked imagination and was always taking the part of the baby while his girlfriends fussed around him and mothered him.

To add to all the changes James encountered that year we also welcomed his sister, Becky, into the world. We waited a few years to have another child as bringing up James had, at times, already felt like we had an additional child in tow. We were concerned about how James would be with Becky, especially his physical behaviour and yes, she did suffer at his hands quite often but equally he could be caring towards her. Poor Becky though never really had a good bedtime routine as James would often hijack that time in the evening. Phil's job saw him being called out and working late at that point so the evening 'routine' was sometimes a solo affair for me.

Throughout this time, James continued to have appointments with doctors, speech therapists, and ear, nose and throat specialists but as ever we got nowhere. The doctor was a good listener and gave us advance prescriptions of antibiotics so that we cold dose James up as soon as we saw an ear infection coming. Other than that, the most he could tell us was that James would probably grow out of the ear infections by the time he was eight. Was this supposed to help us? Four years of his school life would be wasted during this time. Four years of erratic behaviour, of tantrums, of screaming, of making poor progress with his learning. 'He'll grow out of it by the time he is eight' may sound adequate in a textbook but is of little practical use when faced with the actual situation.

James's speech therapy sessions remained few and far between. His speech had greatly improved although I felt this was more from being around other children than from anything the speech therapist may have done. We had now settled into seeing the same speech therapist each time but the fact that she only started looking at James's notes once we walked into the room did not instil my confidence in her. James would sit in her room for a relatively short time and she would seemingly think of something then and there to do with him. She would then suggest something that we could do at home but invariably would not be able to find it in her filing cabinet, so she would find us something she did have filed away to do instead. She was a very nice lady but Phil nearly came to blows with her on one of his visits with James.

James generally performed quite well at speech therapy. He was able to answer some questions appropriately and follow the directions given. However, as I always stated, he was sitting in a quiet room with no distractions. I would have liked him to have been observed at school, with all the associated noises and distractions. This would have given a truer picture of James. As a teacher, I still feel this now when children see a paediatrician in a room with no other distractions. Is this really the best way to see how a child behaves within 'normal' day-to-day life?

Our visits to the Ear, Nose and Throat consultant also became a big bug bear! Whenever James went there his ears were always clear so they could not see a problem. They finally told us that the next time he had an infection we should phone up straight away and he would be seen that week.

In March 2000 James had a particularly bad ear infection. I kept him off school while he screamed for a day. I phoned the hospital that day (Thursday) but they could not see him until a week on Tuesday. In other words, he could be seen in 12 days' time. In our frustration, we tried to get a private appointment but this was going to be even later than the NHS one. We were in a dilemma. Do we keep James off antibiotics so that the ENT consultant can see what he is like or do we give him the medicine? James was in so much pain that we, of course, gave him the antibiotics.

Nursery

I used to play with the massive Teddy bear. I used to look after it with the hospital equipment, with my friend Daniel. I still used to play with Heather then, too.

I did enjoy playing outside on the bikes and other equipment.

*Story-times were boring. I didn't like sitting still and I found it really boring listening to books. They just aren't my thing. I like to **do** things.*

All I remember is making soup there. And that every day after that when my mum picked me up, I went home and asked for vegetable soup – every day for weeks!

Welcome to the World of Education

And so James started Reception class in no better position that when he joined the Nursery. In fact, he now had a reputation as baggage around his neck and his behaviour had certainly got even harder to handle at home especially as he now had a 5-month-old sister to react to and provoke.

James still recalls the teachers who really cared about him at primary school. These were the teachers who listened to him, who gave him time, and who found alternative ways for him to access his learning. He equally remembers the teachers who seemed to make life more difficult for him, the ones who judged too quickly, and the ones who snapped at him before finding out the facts. These were the teachers within whose classes he misbehaved the most, not realising it was because they were expecting him to fit in with everyone else and then becoming frustrated when he just didn't get it or couldn't do it. An open invitation to choose the far more interesting prospect of misbehaving don't you think? Or was it choice? Was James just reacting to the noise, lights, colours, smells, and the other children and this sensory overload was simply taking its toll?

Primary school was difficult. Having to sit and listen for so long when sitting and listening are amongst the most difficult things for you to do. Sitting in noisy dinner halls and assemblies where you sit in close proximity to your peers. And as for the end of each term? Christmas and

Easter, when the normal routine just goes out of the window; they were the times of almost guaranteed mayhem for James.

James had to fight to keep up with everyone at school and we also had to fight his corner throughout his primary school years. Our resolve to fight came in waves and generally involved battling against the system to firstly get him diagnosed and then to get him appropriate support. By the time James had started Reception class we knew there was something more than his hearing affecting his behaviour and learning.

We finally got an appointment with a paediatrician who was rather vague in his summing up but did eventually give James a diagnosis of Dyspraxia and Tourette's syndrome: Dyspraxia because his co-ordination was so poor; Tourette's probably because he spent almost an entire year whistling his way through school and one year making siren noises.

This gave us a starting point but did not seem quite right. I had looked through several books trying to work out what James had and, to be honest, he seemed to have a bit of everything – Dyspraxia, Tourette's, Oppositional Defiance Disorder, Autism, and ADHD, but Autism did seem to tick more boxes than most. In actual fact, I could diagnose myself with some of them and probably most of my family and friends.

Meanwhile James's behaviour continued to go from bad to worse, the gaps in his learning became more evident and he developed many fears and phobias, largely related to noise levels. Fireworks night (and the weeks surrounding it) became unbearable for James so much so that we invested in some ear defenders which he wore even if we went out in the car after dark. Repeating this on New Year's Eve each year then became normal practise as well as every time it thundered.

When James was in Year 2 I started teaching part-time at his school. I was based in the Nursery so actually had very little contact with him as he was at the farthest end of the corridor from me. He did often find his way through to me though if things weren't going right in his classroom. He often appeared at lunchtimes especially when the playground noise proved too much for him. At the end of the day James would meet me in the Nursery and release his frustrations of the day by being verbal or hitting out at me. When I look back now, I'm not quite sure how I coped with those days.

When James was in Year 3, the school applied for Exceptional Needs Funding (ENF) which would provide the school with money to finance 1:1 support for James for several hours per week. Despite a mountain of evidence, James's needs were not deemed great enough for him to receive funding. Neither the school nor I were happy. We appealed and made an appointment to see the Head of SEN at County level. At that point I could understand why so many parents feel that talking to any kind of authority can feel like talking to a brick wall!

I then called upon someone I had met through our local parent led special needs group. She had got her autistic son diagnosed by going to a Harley Street doctor. We got the details and made an appointment. A comprehensive questionnaire arrived both for us and for the school to fill in. It actually had the questions on there that I wanted to talk about. For the first time, I had faith that we were going to see someone who would understand James.

The day of the appointment came, an exciting train ride into London for James, time out of school, and, oh yes, we kept him waiting every time he asked for a drink. Depriving him of a drink may well sound like child cruelty, but instead it was our way of getting him to act in the way he so often would at home. You may remember that waiting was not James's strong point (the Isle of Wight ferry!) and so with every utterance of 'just wait' or 'in a minute' we could almost see him getting more and more agitated. And the result of this? Well, we met in the doctor's office, went through the questionnaires, answered many more questions, and then, bang on cue, James started to explode until the point when he actually tried strangling me. Mission complete!

It is sad to say that when we came out of the clinic with the diagnosis of autism, Phil and I were over the moon. This was not because we had an autistic son. After all, we had already had him for 7 years. The label changed nothing about James, but it did change how people perceived him and how the authorities would view his case.

Strangely enough, James was awarded Exceptional Needs Funding the next time the school applied, followed shortly afterwards by a Statement of Special Educational Needs and the 20 hours support it was then deemed that he required. I look back on this now appreciatively as he would not have been awarded anything in today's inclusive climate. On the other hand, the inclusive nature of schools today might also have seen him having a better school experience than he did.

James had several TAs (Teaching Assistants) who worked with him over the next few years. They were all lovely but some were so nice to him that it didn't really work as he had them wrapped around his little finger. One Teaching Assistant worked with him throughout most of his primary years. She, too, was lovely to him but was also firm and consistent. This relationship worked well. James would often be challenging towards her but she stood her ground and she really cared. He still keeps in contact with her from time to time usually by a Christmas card with a short progress update.

Being Autistic

Being autistic is weird. It gets really annoying because it always has to be me. It's not fair that I am the autistic one and Daniel and Becky aren't.

I don't think anyone ever actually notices it in me. They think I'm just a normal kid really.

I still get really angry at times in my head. At school, this happened a lot. I look alright from the outside but I'm getting angry inside. It's hard to show my autism sometimes because people don't understand. What feels so bad is that I want them to know, but it's hard to tell them because most people don't really know what it is.

I don't think my friends really understood. If they did, then they would know why I acted silly in primary school.

*If anything goes wrong in my life I blame it on my autism. When the chain came off my bike once, I became really depressed because I thought this happened to me because of my autism. Another time, I lost my t-shirt on holiday (it fell off the back of my bike). Again, I blamed it on my autism. After all, it happened to **me** not my brother.*

My mum tries to tell me this is not the case. They are accidents which could happen to anyone. I just can't see this though.

When I See Other Autistic People

I see lots of other autistic children, either at school or in the Special Needs group my family belongs to. I understand there are different spectrums. I watch programs on TV about autistic people too.

I am more able. I've got a lot more to come for me than some of them. They would have to live with someone. They can't really run their own lives when they're older. I feel a bit sad for them.

When I see people more able than me, I feel upset and sad too.

At my secondary school, there were children with other disabilities too. Some were deaf, some had Downs syndrome. I am good around people with more problems because I am used to it. I learned how to use sign language and that was fun.

I didn't have any other autistic children with me at Primary School. There was one boy in my year that had problems. He was like me – he didn't really like school. He left in Year 5 to go to a special school. I've seen him since. We met at a football tournament between our secondary schools. He's doing really well.

Special Friends

We had always talked quite openly with James about why he was having various tests and how this might help him, but it wasn't until he was about nine that we started to use the autism word around him. It seemed fairer for him to know why he was acting the way he did and why he became so angry.

We had already spoken to Daniel about this to help him understand why his brother behaved in the way he did. It didn't actually stop them arguing or falling out, but Daniel revealed his deeper concern and understanding when he was tasked to write a biography while in his final year at Primary school. His teacher was impressed that while others all chose famous people, Daniel chose to write about James. Below are some excerpts from his project:

James

Brooze's

When James gets tantrums he punches and kicks his brother and sister and Sweres Swears. His Mother Jane says "When he does this I send him to the. Stairs for a few minutes".

Favourite food	
1	curry
2	cheese and onion crisps
3	custard cream biscuit

When James gets tantrums he punches and kicks his brother and sister and swears. His mother Jane says "When he does this I send him to the stairs for a few minutes"

Present days

In these days James is in year 4 with Mrs Huges. He has joined old Owens cricket club and has just learnt to swim and ride a bike.

A quote. from his brother Daniel "he may have Problems but he is Still my brother"

In these days James is in Year 4 with Mrs Hughes. He has joined Old Owens cricket club and has learnt to swim and ride a bike.

A quote from his brother Daniel, "he may have problems but he is still my brother"

We had also joined our local parent led special needs group and both boys attended their summer play scheme for several days each year. This was great for Daniel to be spending time with other children who also had siblings with special needs. As Daniel grew older, James continued to attend the play scheme for a few years but this time with Becky. We are still members of this group now and James and Becky particularly have a range of mainstream and special needs friends that they have grown up with. We have been on holiday with them, for days out, taken part in fund-raising days and waved our hands in the air on the annual carnival float. James himself is now a member of the group's committee and is now someone that the younger children look up to. I am sure that many of the long-standing parents in the group would agree with me that we never would have seen that one coming all those years ago!

I have been part of my local special needs group since I was about seven. I started off by going to their play scheme. I was excited about this and I liked going there because it was fun and I went with Dan. I had understanding people looking after me and I made new friends.

The group is a charity, run by parents and aimed at young people and their families. There are lots of other autistic children in the group, as well as visually impaired, Down's syndrome, ADHD, genetic conditions and children in wheelchairs. Some of the people in the group are now our family friends. It feels like we are a big family. We go on trips together and run fund-raising events. The children all help each other out. We push wheel chairs for each other and the older children take the younger children under their wing. Being part of the group made me feel better about myself. People understand me there. I am treated like a person, not someone with a special need. I am glad we joined the group. It has really helped me and I know there are people there that I can turn round to and ask for help.

I have grown up with a lot of the young people in the group. As well as the children with special needs there are lots of their brothers and sisters and we all just mix together. Some of the children feel like they are part of my own family. One boy, Dan, is 3 years younger than me. He is a lovely kid. He has autism and epilepsy. He is very funny and entertaining; he copies lines from films and television programs which makes me laugh. Dan is the eldest in his family so it is harder for him to be independent. I am lucky that I had my Dan as an older brother as he has given me my independence. Dan's brother, Ryan, is 6 years younger than me. Both he and Dan seem like younger brothers to me as I have known them for such a long time. I get on with them really well.

Strangely enough, their step-dad is also one of my best mates. Bob has done a lot for me since I have known him but he is also a very good friend. He is 10 years older than me, but when I go to his house I get on as well with him as I do with Dan and Ryan. Bob used to take me to play football every Sunday but nowadays we are more likely to go for a few beers or to have one of our traditional FIFA nights on the X-Box.

I didn't always get on with everyone. There is one boy, nearly my age, who I didn't get on with for years. We never did, or really have, anything in common until we discovered that we both didn't like another boy at our primary school. This seemed to bring us both together and we get on really well now. His family is also very welcoming and makes me feel part of their family.

So now I am too old to be a child in the group and so I have become a committee member myself. I feel like I can maybe give something back and help with fund-raising and that feels good. The people who started off as my mum's friends are now my friends too.

Feelings

Throughout James's primary years and probably until he was about fourteen he did get very angry and Daniel and Becky were so often on the receiving end of this. Those sibling fights mark everyone's summer, Easter, and Christmas holidays but James was capable of taking these to another level. Not only was he physical (he had that inner strength that many parents of special needs children will know) but his mood could also affect the whole family. When James was angry, everybody in our house (and probably several houses down) knew about it. Swear words would stream from his mouth and there was no quick response to calming him down. On many occasions, I needed to manhandle James, if only to restrain him from hurting someone else or breaking furniture. He would often lash out at me to the point where it no longer seemed to be a big issue but rather just the way things were. Ever since those difficult days, I have never really been fazed by a child in my class becoming physical either. I am not sure that this is a good thing to take in your stride though. The upshot of James's behaviour was that Phil and I became adept at playing good cop / bad cop. We were almost like a tag team stepping in to give each other a much needed break. The lowest moments were when both of us felt defeated at the same time.

From time to time, notes would appear on my bed from James expressing how he felt.

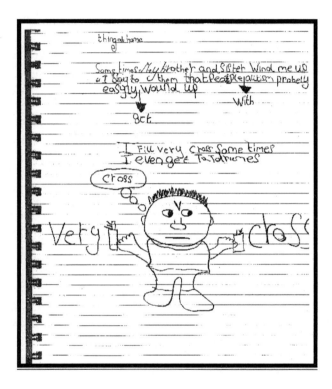

Anger

Sometimes I get so angry. I get easily wound up and then I start swearing. I use swear words a lot.

When I get angry I feel out of control. I feel tense and squidge my fists, and my face feels like it's getting bigger and bubbles up. My head feels like it is spinning inside – it goes round and round and round ...

When I was younger, I used to throw everything round my room, and I hit out at people, especially my mum. I wrote on my bedroom walls and wrote 'kill me' on my mattress and etched it into my mum and dad's bedroom windowsill.

The windowsill etching remained for many years and required careful explanation some years later when we finally had the windows and frames replaced.

The summer of 2009 saw James have a particularly bad meltdown followed by a whole day of his sombre mood. I needed to get away from him for a while so walked to the beach for some rest and recuperation. As ever, my notebook was in my bag. This poem followed.

On the surface, he's like any other
A funny friend, a son, a brother,
A football fan, a boy at school,
An entertainer playing the fool.
But deep down, he just doesn't cope,
Life hits him hard, he gives up hope.
He tries new things but hates the change
He lashes out when things are strange.
"Why me? Why me?" he'll shout at life
As if autism stabbed him with a knife
Whose fault is it? Who is to blame?
He'll say it's me – from me he came.
And when he's calm and the frown is gone
We all forget, we all move on.
On the surface, he's like any other
A funny friend, a son, a brother

Written in August 2009 at Biscarosse beach after a
stressful afternoon of tantrums.

Medics

During James's primary school years, both before and after his diagnosis, we visited a great variety of medics, therapists, healers; whatever you would like to call them.

From the days of being treated as a neurotic parent when I first aired my concerns to taking matters into our own hands to get James diagnosed, we visited many other people on the way. This all cost us a great deal of money, but, as many of you reading this will know, you will do and try anything to help your own child.

We started with Cranial Osteopathy mainly to work on James's ear problems. The main principal of Cranial Osteopathy is to allow the body to make its own changes from within. Through very subtle massage the therapists work with the body aiming to allow the body to self-heal and self-regulate. And so we started the road to realigning James's system into place. After several sessions, even the therapist questioned if there was something else affecting James's behaviour. James did, however, enjoy the sessions, came out seemingly more relaxed, and loved looking through their 'Where's Wally' books each time we went. They even treated me when I turned up with him on one occasion with the most awful chesty cough.

The osteopath also recommended that we visit a specialised orthodontist as James's jaw was out of line and they felt this was putting pressure on certain parts of his sinuses and possibly affecting his ears. In orthodontist terms, this is known as occlusion which describes the contact between the upper and lower teeth. We made the appointment, travelled some distance to get there, and were told that James could be fitted with a special brace which would, over time, stretch and pull his jaw bone into place. Several appointments later, James was keen to get his brace but managed to break it within several weeks of it being fitted. He had a habit of grinding his teeth and this took its toll on the wires. We were told to try again when he was a little bit older but inevitably another treatment came along, and the dentist option became a thing of the past.

I remember going to see Betty. There was a sewing shop near it. I had to have Betty's special 'mashed potato' to get a print of my teeth. I chose a red gum plate. The first time I put it in I didn't like it. I took it out after 30 seconds. On the way back I had some chips. It was really awkward eating them.

Then there was Bob the Brusher, as we called him. I had read about Bob in a magazine and how he used thin brushes to gently brush along nerve pathways which had not developed as they should have. Bob was a Neuro-developmental therapist. He worked on the principal that we all go through a stage of primitive reflexes which have an effect on our postural balance, motor skills learning and social development. For human reflexes to develop normally they have to progress through several stages known as foetal, primitive and adult. If the normal sequence of development is interrupted an individual may fail to grow out of their primitive reflexes and if these reflexes are retained this may lead to a lack of physical, social and emotional integration. Factors which can interrupt the normal sequence of development include shock or stress in pregnancy or childbirth. I had a normal pregnancy with James and most would say a normal birth. The only stress for me was that I arrived at the hospital in the early hours of the morning with contractions and was put on the maternity ward until I became more fully dilated. When the contractions and the pain became more severe, the nurse on the ward more or less told me not to be silly and that I would know when I was in labour. The fact that I had already given birth once obviously did not give me the experience to know this! The upshot was that I was still on the ward, by this time screaming, fully dilated and pushing, and hurriedly taken down to the labour ward in the bed I was already in with only half an hour to go. Phil arrived back at the hospital only 5 minutes before James was born so, yes, I was a little stressed. Would this have impacted on James? I really do not know.

One of the other contributory factors can be toxicity from lead or pesticides. When I was pregnant with James I took advantage of the free dental care that comes with being pregnant and had any outstanding fillings done during this time. I remember talking to the doctors at James's allergy clinic (see next chapter) about whether this could be a contributory factor to James then being tested to reveal mercury in his bloodstream. She agreed that this could be the cause. Exposure to high levels of mercury has been linked to serious nervous system and developmental problems in humans, especially children. I may be clutching at straws here.

I also remember that the water pipes were changed in my home town during my pregnancy. We commented at that time about the water having a strange taste for a while. Could this too have released some chemicals into James's system?

Anyway, the idea of 'brushing' was that by stroking particular sites on the face and body and by practising specific exercises, the nervous system is encouraged to mature. The brushing mimics the movement of these reflexes and eventually makes them progress to the next stage of development. Once these reflexes have progressed there should be a significant change in patterns of behaviour.

And so we started a routine of visiting Bob every few months, of James being tested for progress, and a new program of brushing and exercises being shown to us. It was interesting that Bob said we could see James's retained reflexes by observing how he performed in some exercises. One such exercise was to ask James to walk on the outside edges of his feet. If you or I do this our arms will help us balance with our hands stretched out flat. When James did this his hands completely mimicked his feet and curled into the same position his feet were formed in.

The brushing did seem to have an effect on James. Each set of exercises worked on a different part of his system. Sometimes his behaviour got significantly worse before it started to improve. The biggest impact however was when we worked on the reflexes associated with co-ordination. Within a couple of months, my poorly co-ordinated, tripping-over-nothing son could ride a bike with no stabilisers and catch a ball like a top fielder. Some miracle definitely seemed to have happened there.

We continued with the 'brushing' for about a year when Bob, himself, said he felt we had gone as far as we could with this therapy. James had made progress but any other behaviour was seemingly due to something else.

James was about 6 years old at this point and, as yet, still undiagnosed.

Allergies

During this time of medical visits, I also went to a talk from a doctor from a private hospital about children's allergies and the implications on their behaviour and well-being. This was about more than just the known reactions to an allergy such as a rash or a swollen face. It was about major behavioural and physical reactions to substances which had been in their bodies for a period of time. The talk was fascinating. The doctor seemed to be talking about James.

Once again, we made an appointment and began our journey down this new road. The 'hospital' was actually a private day clinic specialising in the treatment of allergy and environmental illness. James had blood tests, urine tests and stool tests, all of which showed him to have a vast array of metals, and other substances in his body which could be affecting his behaviour. This included having mercury in his bloodstream (as mentioned in the previous chapter) as well as the measles antibody. I will say no more on this subject except that this meant the antibody could travel to his brain and affect his functioning from there.

The principle behind James's treatment was based on the 'load phenomenon' which, in layman terms, is the overburden of some foods or chemicals which we are exposed to every day. The body can take so much exposure to these on a daily basis but a build-up means that the body reaches a threshold above which symptoms occur. James would be tested using allergen-specific-low-dose-immunotherapy (otherwise known as provocation/neutralisation). He would be provoked with intense concentrations of different foods and chemicals, and then given doses of anti-gen which would help to stabilise his responses. The doses of anti-gen given were sequentially lower until a wheal response was seen that did not increase in size.

We spent thousands of pounds on James's treatment and did see some changes. We spent whole days in the hospital while different substances were placed on his tongue and we waited for a reaction. On one occasion, we visited the hospital the day after the school had its 'Mad Hair Day' in aid of Comic Relief. James had spent a day surrounded by hair sprays and hair colours. We did not have a good evening following on from this. The next day he was tested with ethanol. Within a very short space of time he went almost berserk, running around the labs and climbing on my back. It was only when he was given the correct dose of anti-gen by the doctor that he started to calm down.

Despite spending a lot of time and money on this treatment and seeing some positive changes, we could not sustain this financially. We had also tried keeping James on a gluten free diet at this time as well as avoiding other additives advised to us by the hospital. This, too, proved hard to sustain with 3 children all wanting their favourite foods and expensive shopping trips spent looking at labels.

It is possible that you are reading this thinking why on earth did you try so many treatments. Think of one of your own children. What wouldn't you do to improve their lives?

My Funny Ways!

My autism makes me do some strange things, but some of them are quite useful.

I am very organised in some ways. I get everything organised for school the night before so that I am completely ready for the morning. I also like making lists, especially when I go on holiday. I really don't like leaving anything behind.

Whenever I go out, but especially when we go away, I check my bedroom lots of times. I close the curtains, hide any valuables away, unplug electrical items and shut the door tight. Years ago, someone I thought was a friend stole from my bedroom. I think this is what made me worry about security.

Over the years, I have done some other very strange things too.

At one time, I kept asking my mum 'What's the time in Australia?' and another time I kept asking 'How old are you?' Mum said I did this every time I seemed unsure of anything. They were like fail-safe questions that would bring everything back to normality again. Around this time, the doctors also thought I had Tourette's syndrome. This was before I was diagnosed with Autism.

When I was in Year 1 at primary school I whistled, and whistled, and whistled. Apparently, I did this for about a year. Once I whistled in assembly (I didn't know I was doing this) and I got told off. I used to get told off a lot for being naughty and sometimes I was sent to the Head teacher. This was before I was diagnosed with Autism.

There are some other habits too that have irritated other people. I used to go to a hospital for allergy testing and we would spend the whole day in a small room with a DVD player. I watched the film 'Babe' over and over and over again. I didn't watch it any other time, just for the whole day when we went to the hospital. Either my mum or dad sat with me each of these days. Neither of them ever wants to watch 'Babe' again and say they were really glad when I started watching the 'Shrek' DVD instead.

One last habit: I used to <u>love</u> having a bath. Sometimes I would have 2 baths in one night. They were nice and hot, and I felt nice and relaxed. I like the heat, especially in the winter time. I still like water now. When I swim I feel really relaxed.

Secondary School

In 2005 we had to start thinking about where James should go to secondary school. He could join Daniel at one of our local schools or we could choose for him to attend a special school. As James had a Statement of Special Educational Needs we had a degree of say as to which way his future would go.

Our decision was based on more than just academic learning. James's levels were well below average but were only on the borderline of the levels required for a child to attend a special school. With more recent changes in inclusive policy, James would have had no chance of attending a special school in today's educational climate. His academic ability, though still deemed to be well below average for his ability, would be way above the threshold to be considered for a special school.

Our main driver for seeking special school education for James was the desire to see his raised self-esteem; to see him feel like he was achieving and to see him learning the skills that he would eventually need to succeed in life. James himself, wanted to go to secondary school with his friends but with three schools to choose from in our area I knew there was a distinct possibility that he could end up at a school with none of his friends.

I had also seen how the right teacher had made a positive difference to James's well-being and the detrimental effect that a less inclusive teacher could have. Mainstream schooling would see James moving from one lesson to another with a different teacher for each lesson. The law of probability said to me that each day he would be likely to meet teachers who did not understand autism and whose patience and teaching style was not going to welcome James in with open arms. He would find himself in the bottom set for everything with the potential for being with some peers who did not really want to be educated. This furthered the chances of him getting in with the wrong crowd, getting into trouble, feeling like the world was against him, lowering his self-esteem and so on.

The alternative was a school for children with moderate learning difficulties and with autistic provision. This school was a half hour taxi ride away but the teachers had chosen to work there knowing they would be with children with special needs. James would learn life skills and social skills and qualifications were offered even if not at GCSE level. He would not stand out at this school. He would not have special needs. He would just be James.

With James's increasingly depressive mood about school and his destructive feelings becoming ever more apparent, we felt that we would be doing him a disservice not to try getting him into the special school.

James will say that we took him away from his friends and, yes, this was a downside (although they did all go different schools as predicted). For me, it was the best decision we ever made. The constant feeling of fighting for James's rights seemed to subside the minute he walked through that door.

The following 2 notes were written by James in his final
year at primary school.

Dear mum

I'm Lost and have destroyed my life.
You may be my mum, but im not your
child. I need help help!!!!!! I'm scared
of my own Family its becuse I'm having
a bad time School. I maybe have
Problems yes Knowbody likes
me mum you like me Plus The
Whole world dont I Like me

I'm sorry but this
might make you Chie

This is why we needed a fresh start.

When I left my primary school, my mum made me go to a Special School. She thought this would be the best place for me to go. A small part of me wanted to go because it sounded good. It said it had a cricket pitch. I thought it would help me to be independent. I thought people would understand me more.

I didn't want to go because I wouldn't see my primary school friends anymore. Before I went I was really nervous. I didn't want to go and on the first day I had a big tantrum and lay there for ages and kicked and screamed. I was nearly in tears when the taxi came to get me. The first day was good though.

I remember I was in a taxi and John, the Escort, gave me a tour of all the places on the way. I went into my Family group. I had already met Paul in the taxi and he was in my form with me too. Our tutor came to meet us in the playground. Only me and Paul were in my form that day as it was a special day for Year Sevens. My form tutors were all nice. I came home happy that day equipped with a diary and a starter pack.

The second day came and I was really nervous again. Everyone else was back at school that day and there were big children in the corridor. I felt really small and scared. At first I really liked all the teachers. Some of them were really funny. They listened to me. I could have a proper conversation with them and they respected me for who I was.

In Year Nine things changed a little. I had a new teacher who I got on well with at first. He seemed funny but somehow his jokes just didn't always work. He didn't understand that his humour did not always work for people with autism. He also had one rule for himself and one rule for everyone else. I HATE injustice. I had been fine at my school before because there were rules and I knew where I stood. I knew what I could and couldn't do and that worked for me.

Once things started to become unfair, I found it hard to cope. I felt that this teacher was popular with everyone else so I thought that everyone else was against me too.

Everything just went pear shaped. I started causing trouble such as swearing at teachers, and walking out of class which meant I ended up in isolation and had to change Family groups. It was only because my first tutors cared for me and fought hard to get me back, that I was allowed back to my original group.

My Head of Year also looked out for me at this time. I thought he was really scary at first but he turned out to be a big help. I knew I could talk to him whenever I needed to and he helped me to find solutions to my problems.

In my last year at school I also saw a Counsellor. This was a big help and it changed my mind over what I thought about school and how I felt for the future. On my first session, I wrote down all the pros and cons about school and my teachers. On my last session, I screwed it up, put it in the bin and said, "Now, this is the future".

By the time I left school I was nervous to go. I was sad to leave particular teachers. We had a Prom and I really didn't want to go. My teachers persuaded me with about a week to go. I'm glad I went as I really enjoyed it. On our Leavers' Day I spoke to Governors and Examiners about some of the work I had done for my exams. I was confident and I think I did well. I had some positive feedback. I left secondary school with my head held high.

Back Out Into The World

James did do well at his secondary school. He left with 5 GCSEs and other Entry level awards. He became a Sports Ambassador, went on a trip away to France, made some good friends and was well-liked by the staff. He was in the top group in his year group which immediately saw the raising of his self-esteem. He won awards for best in class at particular subjects and played the drums in the school concert. Parents' evenings were a pleasure to attend.

Yes, he did still have his fair share of problems there but had enough understanding staff to turn his negatives into positives. His Head of Year used to take him out on a bike ride when things got too much for him in school. What a brilliant way to calm him down!

Did I do the right thing sending him to a special school? When I look at the young man now who holds his own at college, travels independently by bus and train, handles his own bank account and has held down several part-time jobs, a resounding 'YES' comes over me. You will see towards the end of this book especially that James does not necessarily agree this was the right decision. I don't think we will ever really know whether mainstream or special education would have given him a better grounding for all aspects of life. They certainly both have their merits and pitfalls.

I'm going to college soon. I'm quite excited because it's something new and I feel ready for it. I'm a little bit nervous as well because it's something new. It's going to be more crowded than school with more new people.

I'm looking forward to having a life. It's like an extra step, isn't it? I'm going to do carpentry and football training as part of my course.

Dan is going to University. That will be weird and strange (but I also get the X-box to myself). I'm so used to having him around. I will miss the banter and he would help me if I need a hand with something. Plus I could go and visit him.

Hobbies

James's main concern about attending a special school was being taken away from the 'friends' he had made at his primary school. It was therefore always of great importance that he had other mainstream activities in his free time.

James had played cricket for the school team while at primary school. Since the days of his body brushing he had become a skilled ball catcher and when he hit the ball he could bat it with such gusto that it would inevitably go far. One of our neighbours coached at the local cricket club so James started training with him weekly. Although he was mixing with mainstream peers James still found it difficult to join in with the others and would stand back looking a little awkward. Before long he started playing in matches. (At this point I discovered that the benefits of being a cricket mum as opposed to a football mum are the increased chance of warm weather and a club house). We drove around the County finding well hidden cricket grounds but I cannot begin to tell you about the anxiety level that would exude from James in that car. On one occasion I thought he would not play he was so nervous and so near to tears. I managed to beckon over my neighbour, we jollied James along and he took up his position to field. Well, considering the state he was in I was astounded when he achieved the catch of the day by quite literally diving to get the ball. His cricket whites were never quite the same again but that grass stain told a story and his self-esteem had a little boost too. Despite some successes over the few years James played, he chose not to continue when my neighbour stopped coaching there. He spoke to the other boys but still felt like the outsider and the relationships were not strong enough to keep him there.

James's other hobby has long been supporting Tottenham Hotspur. Being able to talk about football immediately gave James an access into conversations with his mainstream peers and, I always felt, stood him in good stead for spending time at the pub when he was older. After relying on me so heavily when he was in his primary years, football matches suddenly gave the biggest boost ever to the father /son relationship between James and Phil. Following years of wanting me to accompany him everywhere and Phil not really getting a look in, we now had an activity that had nothing to do with me; an activity that only Phil could support him with.

Tottenham

I used to support Liverpool Football Club. We even went to visit their stadium at Anfield once when I was younger. My Dad supported Spurs and my brother supported Arsenal. One day I went to White Hart Lane to see Spurs V Birmingham with my dad and his friend, John. From that point on I supported Spurs, partly because I realised I lived too far away to ever go to Liverpool matches.

When I first started going to football matches, I was really nervous. I didn't like going. I just wanted to go home. I didn't like being in a crowd. I kept asking my dad "What's the time?" all the time. It became one of my security sayings.

When I was 11, I became a Spurs member and at 14 I got a season ticket. I had got used to being in that particular type of crowd and felt comfortable with the atmosphere. I knew where everything was and how to get to White Hart Lane from home. Being a season ticket holder also means that I now know exactly which stand I will be in and, even better, exactly where I will be sitting. I know the people around me and chat to them each match day.

I feel good being a Spurs supporter and feel dedicated to the team. I don't think about being autistic when I am there as I am no different to anyone else. I like to join in with the crowd and the atmosphere. I also like it as I often meet up with my friends, Dan and Matt, at half-time. Matt was my friend all through primary school until we went to separate schools when we were 11.

Moving On

James was growing up which was a scary prospect. For the past few years he had attended a school where his individual needs had largely been catered for. There was a sense of security surrounding him for those 5 years and a feeling in me that I no longer needed to fight his corner all of the time; other people had taken up that mantle and done it for me. So what would the future bring? It felt like James was finally entering the big bad world, a place where his autism might once again set him apart as having a special need.

James left secondary school in a good place. He now had well-developed social skills, greater confidence, strategies to cope with his anger, and a string of achievements under his belt.

A few weeks into his college course we met with James's tutor. She was really impressed with him and found it hard to believe that he had been to a special school as he was out-performing some of the children from mainstream schools, both socially and academically. I wonder if he would have been in such a position if he too had attended a mainstream school.

Unbeknown to his tutor though, there were many parts of his day that were playing on his mind and causing him some anxiety but he was covering these up well while at college.

Moving on from school was scary. I was going to college and I hoped it would build my confidence. I hoped that the course would help me get a life and a career. I wanted to do carpentry but I didn't feel independent enough to do the actual carpentry course.

The course I did was an all-round one. I did English, Maths, ICT, Carpentry, Football training, and Art. It was a course specifically for people like me. A lot of other students had either come from special schools or had been in the lower sets at their mainstream schools. I wanted to learn though and not everyone there did.

I expected more of a free life and I did get that there and I did become more independent. The course wasn't exactly what I expected. I found my confidence in the first three months and then thought I don't really need this anymore. I felt that I was repeating some of the things I had already done at school. I didn't feel I could get much more from the course.

The college was a very busy place. There seemed to be too much going on with different people coming and going every day. I didn't like some of the people there. Some of the other students were more streetwise and I didn't feel as safe and secure as I did at school. Also, the schedules were just not as organised as they had been at school. Lessons would change at the last minute or we couldn't do carpentry because the room had been booked out to someone else. I found this quite difficult at times.

I did move on that year though. It took me a while to settle into college life. It was a big change from school.

But I did make some friends and it did bridge the gap between school and the college I attend now.

James successfully completed his year at college with his biggest achievement being that he now felt ready to tackle a mainstream course at a different college. I will let James tell you the rest.

I went to my first college wanting to do carpentry but during that year I changed my mind. Whenever we went to watch Spurs play I was always really impressed with the way they kept their pitch so my mind started to change to think about Grounds-keeping. My mum's friend recommended a Horticultural college nearby so that's where I chose to go next. I enrolled to do a Level 1 Diploma in Horticulture.

The college is a friendly place and everyone seems happy. People have come to the college because they know what they want to do, not just to fill time. The tutors are caring and take time to speak to you about your career. This is my first time being a part of a mainstream course. I am treated with respect and the whole class get on with each other.

When I first started, I was very nervous and very quiet. A few months in though I started to know more people and to make some friends. The course is practical which suits me, but even when I do written work, I understand why I am learning these things. I've learned to fall in love with the work I'm doing and I care about my work because the people around me care.

And as for the future? Well, I feel nervous. It's a big change from being sixteen to eighteen. At school, you just move on from year to year and don't really have to think about what the next year will bring. At eighteen, I have learnt that it's you who has to pick what you want to do. Making decisions is quite scary.

Turning Eighteen

So, our teenage son with special needs started to turn into the adult we would never have imagined all those years ago. His 18th birthday came and went. We had a gathering of friends which turned out to be about 40-50 people. James chatted to everyone with confidence. That same year he got a temporary gardening job, took on some private gardening work, happily going to meet his new clients on his own and he got a distinction in his Level 1 Diploma in Horticulture. Oh yes, and he also got voted 'Best Student' on his course. His citation read:

'James has been awarded this prize based on the excellent feedback given from his peers, tutors and learning support team. James has grown in confidence throughout this year and now confidently takes the team leader role on practicals when required where he leads his team with organisation, fairness and motivation. James makes a great effort with his course work and assignments and sets himself high expectations. This in turn has inspired several of his class mates who have seen the standard of his work and then wanted to do as well as James. I am personally delighted to see him win this award, I am very proud of this young man who I am sure will progress well in Level 2 Horticulture and even eventually onto a Level 3, something he did not feel he could ever achieve before he came to Capel.'

As the Awards ceremony began, the loud speakers played 'Hall of Fame' by The Script. How true the words of that song were and how proud I felt. If I could pinpoint James's life with the lyrics of a song, then this is where we were at that exact moment.

Yeah, you can be the greatest

You can be the best

You can be the King Kong banging on your chest

You can beat the world

You can beat the war

You can talk to God

Go banging on his door

You can throw your hands up

You can beat the clock (yeah)

You can move a mountain

You can break rocks

You can be a master

Don't wait for luck

Dedicate yourself and you gon' find yourself

Standing in the hall of fame (yeah)

And the world's gonna know your name (yeah)

'Cause you burn with the brightest flame (yeah)

And the world's gonna know your name (yeah)

And you'll be on the walls of the hall of fame

You can go the distance

You can run the mile

You can walk straight through hell with a smile

You can be the hero

You can get the gold

Breaking all the records they thought never could be broke

Yeah, do it for your people

Do it for your pride

How are you ever gonna know if you never even try?

Do it for your country

Do it for your name

'Cause there's gonna be a day...

When you're standing in the hall of fame (yeah)

And the world's gonna know your name (yeah)

'Cause you burn with the brightest flame (yeah)

And the world's gonna know your name (yeah)

And you'll be on the walls of the hall of fame

James went on to complete his Level 2 Diploma in Horticulture, again gaining a distinction and being voted best student on his course.

Social Skills

Just one last thought before I bring this book to a close. Despite all of James's successes – his awards, his exams, his work ethic, the way he has turned himself round to become a positive role model, there is still one aspect of life which he perceives himself to find difficult. I say 'perceives' because I now see James as someone who can talk to a range of people, be really quite entertaining and communicate with his colleagues at work. However, James feels that he still finds social situations difficult.

Going out has always been hard for me as I'm not the most sociable person you will meet. I find it hard to socialise as I'm very self-conscious.

Going from a mainstream primary to a special needs secondary school, personally hit me very hard. I find it hard to talk to people who have gone to mainstream school. I feel like I don't fit in with them. I'm not up to date and I don't feel capable of what they are capable of. I feel this has also made me unsociable in my home town. I just wanted what everyone else had at that age such as going out and being invited to parties. I feel like going to a special needs school took this away from me and took a bit of normality out of me. I still find it hard now. I try to go out but then I get that nervous, self-conscious feeling again.

When I turned eighteen I thought a lot would change but when I look back at it, eighteen is just a number and another year. I feel that going to a special needs school has helped me with the academic side of things and I did learn lots of social skills, but when it comes to being sociable, I feel absolutely clueless. I just want to have a group of friends in my own home town, like my brother did.

I look at my sister now who is 15 and every weekend she is doing something. At this age, I wish I could have gone out with friends but I felt I didn't know anyone as I went to school a half hour drive from where I live. At the age of 15, I felt that I had completely lost contact with my friends from primary school.

The things is, I probably wouldn't have still been friends with many of my primary school friends even if I had gone to school in my home town but maybe I would have made a couple of new friends. I did make friends at my special school but they lived too far away.

When I don't get invited places, I feel lonely and worthless. I find New Year's Eve particularly difficult. I feel angry and upset because I want to do something on New Year's Eve but I don't know anyone in my home town anymore, or at least they don't see me as someone they would want to invite out.

On one of those traumatic New Year's Eves, when James was feeling particularly down, he said,

"I know I am a good person and I have a good heart but where does that get me?"

December 2013

Well, James, it gets you through college with Distinctions, it gets you an apprenticeship, and it gets you people who love you and other children who look up to you. If you want to know where it gets you, look back at how far you have come. It gets you as far as you strive for.

Reflections

And so it's the last day of the holiday. My notebook is with me and most of the book is now written in rough. I have typed some of it up as the years have passed but there is still a long way to go. I really need to seize this moment, sat on the beach, looking out to sea, the warm sun on my skin, and move forward from this point. The time has come to close this book, at least for now. Eighteen summer holidays have taken us on the most amazing and fulfilling journey. It's time to enjoy the view now. I wonder what the next chapters of our lives will bring. Oh, and do you remember I wrote about James struggling with the noise of fireworks and thunder? Well, on our 18th summer holiday we went to watch 'Beach on Fire', an impressive firework display along the coastline near Venice. Although James jumped at the first bang, he stayed, calmly took photos, and then coped admirably as we walked back from the beach through the start of a thunderstorm. A fitting end to the 18th summer holiday I think.

And to all the people who ever crossed my path with James – all the glances, and sighs, and hidden comments. The strangers who looked at us in shops, the friends and family whose faces said 'Why can't you control your child?' I forgive you. It would be too hard to go through life feeling bitter and, after all, if I had never been given the opportunity to have James in my life, would I have been doing the same?

Forgiveness is one thing but, I do not forget. I can recall every tut, every nuance of body language, every awkward silence, every futile piece of advice I have ever been given from so many people who just didn't understand. I remember all those who suddenly miraculously seemed to find a certain patience and sympathy for James once he had received his diagnosis, and who instantly felt themselves to be experts on autism simply because they were part of our lives.

I am no expert on autism myself and without finding out about an individual, could not advise others as all autistic children are so different. I am an expert on James though and I know that despite what people may have thought, I now have a charming, amusing, street-wise son, who I am immensely proud of. We must have done something right then!

And to those of you who have been blessed with a similarly challenging but inspirational child, my advice to you would be to take one day at a time. In those dark early days, I never would have imagined having the son I have now.

And finally, during the year that James visited the allergy clinic, this record was released. The words gave me hope that everything would, in time, be okay and that James could, in time, achieve and be brilliant. I played this in the car each time we drove to the clinic and it spurred me on to continue fighting for what could be. The words of this song still inspire me today.

I am a mountain

I am a tall tree, oh

I am a swift wind

Sweepin' the country

I am a river

Down in the valley, oh

I am a vision

And I can see clearly

If anybody asks you who I am

Just stand up tall

Look 'em in the face and say

I'm that star up in the sky

I'm that mountain peak up high

Hey, I made it

I'm the world's greatest

And I'm that little bit of hope

When my back's against the ropes

I can feel it

I'm the world's greatest

I am a giant

I am an eagle, oh

I am a lion

Down in the jungle

I am a marchin' band

I am the people, oh

I am a helpin' hand

I am a hero,

In the ring of life, I'll reign love

And the world will notice a king

When there is darkness I'll shine a light

And mirrors of success reflect in me

I saw the light

At the end of a tunnel

Believe in the pot of gold

At the end of the rainbow

And faith was right there

To pull me through, yeah

Used to be locked doors

Now I can just walk on through

I'm that star up in the sky

I'm that mountain peak up high

Hey, I made it

I'm the world's greatest

I'm that little bit of hope

When my back's against the ropes

I can feel it

I'm the world's greatest

This book has been written on the beaches of France and Italy – Palmyre, Lacanau, Venice, Biscarosse, Pierre Lefitte, Peschierra. Summer holidays are a great time to talk.